This edition copyright © 2003 Lion Publishing
Illustrations copyright © 2003 Debbie Lush

Published by
**Lion Publishing plc**
Mayfield House, 256 Banbury Road,
Oxford OX2 7DH, England
www.lion-publishing.co.uk
ISBN 0 7459 4665 8

First edition 2003
1 3 5 7 9 10 8 6 4 2 0

**Acknowledgments**

6: 'The Painting Lesson' by Trevor Harvey, from *Funny Poems* ed.
Heather Amery, published 1990 by Usborne. 8: 'Ten Things Mums
Never Say', from *Dad, You're Not Funny* by Steve Turner, copyright
© 1999 Steve Turner, published by Lion Publishing plc. Used by
permission. 13: Luke 1:46–49, from the Good News Bible published
by The Bible Societies/HarperCollins Publishers Ltd, UK © American
Bible Society 1966, 1971, 1976, 1992, used with permission. 14, 20:
'Independence' and 'Disobedience', from *When We Were Very Young*
copyright © A.A. Milne. Copyright under the Berne Convention.
Published by Egmont Books Ltd, London, and used with permission.
16: 'Purple Shoes' by Irene Rawnsley, from *Read Me*, published 1998
by Macmillan. 28: 'I Am Becoming My Mother', from *I Am Becoming
My Mother* by Lorna Goodison, published 1986 by New Beacon
Books Ltd. Used by permission. 29: 'Like a Beacon', from *The Fat
Black Woman's Poems* by Grace Nichols, copyright © 1984 Grace
Nichols, published by Virago Press. Used by permission.
Every effort has been made to trace and acknowledge copyright
holders of all the quotations in this book. We apologize for any errors
or omissions that may remain, and would ask those concerned to
contact the publishers, who will ensure that full acknowledgment
is made in the future.

A catalogue record for this book is available
from the British Library

Typeset in 10/15 Verdana
Printed and bound in Singapore

# *About* *Mothers*

ILLUSTRATED BY
*Debbie Lush*

# Child's Eye View

## The Painting Lesson

'What's THAT, dear?'
asked the new teacher.
'It's Mummy,' I replied.
'But mums aren't green and orange!
You really haven't TRIED.
You don't just paint in SPLODGES
– You're old enough to know
You need to THINK before you work...
Now – have another go.'
She helped me draw two arms and legs,
A face with sickly smile,
A rounded body, dark brown hair,
A hat – and, in a while,
She stood back (with her face bright pink):
'That's SO much better – don't you think?'
But she turned white
At ten to three
When an orange-green blob
Collected me.
'Hi, Mum!'

Trevor Harvey

## Ten Things Mums Never Say

1. Keep your mouth open when you eat,
   then you'll be able to talk at the same time.

2. Jump down the stairs.
   It's quicker than walking.

3. Don't eat all your vegetables.
   You won't have enough room for your sweets.

4. It's too early for bed.
   Stay up and watch more television.

5. Be rude to your teachers.
   It would be dishonest to be polite.

6. By all means walk on the furniture.
   It's already badly scratched.

7. Don't brush your teeth.
   They'll only get dirty again.

8. It's not your fault that your pocket money
   only lasts for a day.

9. Wipe your feet on the sofas.
   That's what they're there for.

10. I was far worse behaved than you
    when I was young.

**Steve Turner**

*Parents should conduct their arguments in quiet, respectful tones, but in a foreign language. You'd be surprised what an inducement that is to the education of children.*

**Judith Martin**

*The value to a child of poor role models is underestimated. Parents have the idea that it is their duty to set a good example, never realizing that a bad one will do just as well, indeed better.*

**Jill Tweedie**

# Mother Love

## The Little Boy Found

The little boy lost in the lonely fen,
Led by the wandering light,
Began to cry; but God, ever nigh,
Appeared like his father in white.

He kissed the child, and by the hand led,
And to his mother brought,
Who in sorrow pale, through the lonely dale,
Her little boy weeping sought.

**William Blake**

## The Truest Friend

A mother is the truest friend we have,
when trials, heavy and sudden, fall upon us;
when adversity takes the place of prosperity;
when friends who rejoice with us in our sunshine
desert us when troubles thicken around us,
still will she cling to us,
and endeavour by her kind precepts and counsels
to dissipate the clouds of darkness,
and cause peace to return to our hearts.

Washington Irving

*'O! help me, heaven,' she prayed, 'to be decorative
and to do right!'*

Ronald Firbank

# Aurora Leigh

Women know
The way to rear up children (to be just),
They know a simple, merry, tender knack
Of tying sashes, fitting baby shoes,
And stringing pretty words that make no sense.
Which things are corals to cut life upon,
Although such trifles: children learn by such.

**Elizabeth Barrett Browning**

# Song of Praise

My heart praises the Lord;
my soul is glad because of God my Saviour,
for he has remembered me, his lowly servant!
From now on all people will call me happy,
because of the great thing the Mighty God
      has done for me.

**Mary, mother of Jesus**

# Battling It Out

## Independence

I never did, I never did, I never *did* like
'Now take care, dear!'
I never did, I never did, I never *did* want
'Hold-my-hand;'
I never did, I never did, I never *did* think much of
'Not up there, dear!'
It's no good saying it. They don't understand.

A.A. Milne

*The joys of motherhood are never fully experienced
until the children are in bed.*

**Author unknown**

*I did not throw myself into the struggle for life:
I threw my mother into it.*

**George Bernard Shaw**

## *Purple Shoes*

Mum and me had a row yesterday,
a big, exploding
howdareyouspeaktomelikethatI'mofftostayatGran's
kind of row.

It was about shoes.
I'd seen a pair of purple ones at Carter's,
heels not too high, soft suede, silver buckles;
'No,' she said.
'Not suitable for school.
I can't afford to buy rubbish.'
That's when we had our row.
I went to bed longing for those shoes.
They made footsteps in my mind,
kicking up dance dust;
I wore them in my dreams across a shiny floor,
under flashing coloured lights.
It was ruining my life not to have them.

This morning they were mine.
Mum relented and gave me the money.
I walked out of the store wearing new purple shoes.
I kept seeing myself reflected in shop windows
with purple shoes on,
walking to the bus stop,
walking the whole length of our street
wearing purple shoes.

On Monday I shall go to school in purple shoes.
Mum will say no a thousand furious times
But I don't care.
I'm not going to give in.

**Irene Rawnsley**

# Separation

## To My Mother

Most near, most dear, most loved and most far,
Under the window where I often found her
Sitting as huge as Asia, seismic with laughter,
Gin and chicken helpless in her Irish hand,
Irresistible as Rabelais, but most tender for
The lame dogs and hurt birds that surround her –
She is a procession no one can follow after
But be like a little dog following a brass band.

She will not glance up at the bomber, or condescend
To drop her gin and scuttle to a cellar,
But lean on the mahogany table like a mountain
Whom only faith can move, and so I send
O all my faith and all my love to tell her
That she will move from mourning into morning.

George Barker

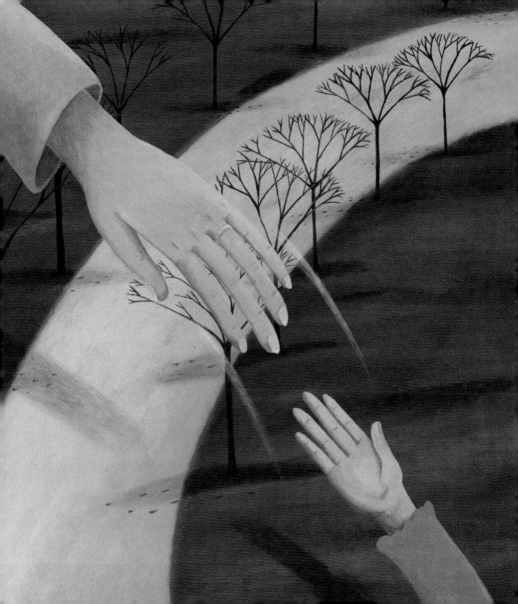

# Disobedience

James James
Morrison Morrison
Weatherby George Dupree
Took great
Care of his Mother,
Though he was only three.
James James
Said to his Mother,
'Mother,' he said, said he;
'You must never go down to the end of the town,
if you don't go down with me.'

James James
Morrison's Mother
Put on a golden gown,
James James
Morrison's Mother
Drove to the end of the town.
James James
Morrison's Mother
Said to herself, said she:
'I can get right down to the end of the town
and be back in time for tea.'

King John
Put up a notice,
'LOST or STOLEN or STRAYED!
JAMES JAMES
MORRISON'S MOTHER
SEEMS TO HAVE BEEN MISLAID.
LAST SEEN
WANDERING VAGUELY:
QUITE OF HER OWN ACCORD,
SHE TRIED TO GET DOWN TO THE END OF THE TOWN –
FORTY SHILLINGS REWARD!'

James James
Morrison Morrison
(Commonly known as Jim)
Told his
Other relations
Not to go blaming *him*.
James James
*Said* to his Mother,
'Mother,' he said, said he:
'You must *never* go down to the end of the town
without consulting me.'

A.A. Milne

# Being There

## Always With You

Your mother is always with you.
She's the whisper of the leaves
as you walk down the street.
She's the smell of bleach
in your freshly laundered socks.
She's the cool hand on your brow
when you're not well.
Your mother lives inside your laughter.
She's crystallized in every teardrop.
She's the place you came from,
your first home.
She's the map you follow
with every step that you take.
She's your first love
and your first heartbreak...
and nothing on earth can separate you.

**Author unknown**

## *Motherhood*

She laid it where the sunbeams fall
Unscanned upon the broken wall.
Without a tear, without a groan,
She laid it near a mighty stone,
Which some rude swain had haply cast
Thither in sport, long ages past,
And Time with mosses had o'erlaid,
And fenced with many a tall grass blade,
And all about bid roses bloom
And violets shed their soft perfume.
There, in its cool and quiet bed,
She set her burden down and fled:
Nor flung, all eager to escape,
One glance upon the perfect shape
That lay, still warm and fresh and fair,
But motionless and soundless there.

And there it might have lain forlorn
From morn till eve, from eve to morn:
But that, by some wild impulse led,
The mother, ere she turned and fled,
One moment stood erect and high;
Then poured into the silent sky
A cry so jubilant, so strange,
That Alice – as she strove to range
Her rebel ringlets at her glass –
Sprang up and gazed across the grass;
Shook back those curls so fair to see,
Clapped her soft hands in childish glee;
And shrieked – her sweet face all aglow,
Her very limbs with rapture shaking –
'My hen has laid an egg, I know;
And only hear the noise she's making!'

**Charles Stuart Calverley**

# Memory

## Piano

Softly, in the dusk, a woman is singing to me;
Taking me back down the vista of years, till I see
A child sitting under the piano, in the boom
    of the tingling strings
And pressing the small, poised feet of a mother
    who smiles as she sings.

In spite of myself, the insidious mastery of song
Betrays me back, till the heart of me weeps to belong
To the old Sunday evenings at home, with winter outside
And hymns in the cosy parlour, the tinkling piano our guide.

So now it is vain for the singer to burst into clamour
With the great black piano appassionato. The glamour
Of childish days is upon me, my manhood is cast
Down in the flood of remembrance, I weep like a child
    for the past.

**D.H. Lawrence**

# I Am Becoming My Mother

Yellow/brown woman
fingers smelling always of onions

My mother raises rare blooms
and waters them with tea
her birth waters sang like rivers
my mother is now me

My mother had a linen dress
the colour of the sky
and stored lace and damask
tablecloths
to pull shame out of her eye.

I am becoming my mother
brown/yellow woman
fingers smelling always of onions.

Lorna Goodison

## *Like a Beacon*

In London
every now and then
I get this craving
for my mother's food
I leave art galleries
in search of plantains
saltfish/sweet potatoes

I need this link

I need this touch
of home
swinging my bag
like a beacon
against the cold

**Grace Nichols**